31 Days
of
Poetry Prompts
for
young poets

Jim Russo

& Nita

ACKNOWLEDGMENTS

A big shout out to :

Poetry Santa Cruz
Willow Glen Poetry Project of San Jose
Sparring with Beatnik Ghosts of Santa Cruz

Author photo on back cover by Todd Russo

Author inquiries and mail orders:

Available on amazon.com

Sky Bolt Circus Press
2510 Soquel Ave, Suite 211
Santa Cruz, CA 95062

facebook.com/CentralCoastPoetryShows
www. CentralCoastPoetryShows.com

OTHER BOOKS BY THIS AUTHOR

Soldiers for Peace & Kids Ruled

Sway of Color & Laura

I Wanna Hold Your Hand & Make Your Move

***

31 Days of Poetry Prompts: Grief & Loss

31 Days of Poetry Prompts: Humanity

31 Days of Poetry Prompts: Love & Romance

31 Days of Poetry Prompts: Reflections

Presently the younger generation

will come knocking at my door.

-Henrik Ibsen

THE MASTER BUILDER

INTRODUCTION

31 Days of Poetry Prompts is part journal, part workbook, and a whole lot of fun. Sit down and relax, we did the hard part, we removed the blank page that seems to block creativity, so now all you have to do is be inspired by the daily prompts.

Poetry Prompts can be used literally as a line in your poem, or as a jumping off place with a slight twist—these Prompts are designed to be evocative and inspirational.

For a unique challenge, for each prompt write poems in different poetic forms try a limerick, a ghazel and a tanka for one prompt; and a spoken word, sonnet and haiku for another.

We've provided extra pages at the end so you can experiment with your own prompts.

We hope you enjoy this series.

Day 3 Prompt: **Playing in the street**

 The truth about parents…

Day 10 Prompt: **First day of summer**

Day 11 Prompt: **Finding out someone you respect is wrong**

Day 13 Prompt: **Say goodbye to someone you don't want to leave**

Day 14 Prompt: **3-5 objects that tell the story of you**

Day 14 Prompt: **3-5 objects that tell the story of you**

Day 16 Prompt: **Use a line from a favorite movie or book as your first line**

Day 16 Prompt: **Use a line from a favorite movie or book as your first line**

Day 19 Prompt: **A poem about an object written in the shape of that object: a cloud poem in the shape of a cloud, a tree poem in the shape of a tree…**

 Then and now. Compare and contrast how it used to be with how it is now

Day 22 Prompt: **I am small now, but when I get bigger…**

Day 22 Prompt: **I am small now, but when I get bigger…**

 Invent a word and use it in a poem using only context to define it

 Be your own shadow—write about your day in the 3rd person

Day 29 Prompt: **Shared secrets**

Day 29 Prompt: **Shared secrets**

Now write some more!

ABOUT THE AUTHOR

Jim is a narrative poet, a storyteller with a sense of humor. Jim believes it's every artist's calling to observe and comment.

He is host of the local TV show— Central Coast Poetry Shows.